The Fire Behind My Eyes

Dawnell Harrison

The Fire Behind My Eyes

A collection of the poetry of
Dawnell Harrison

Idaho USA

Published by Rodent Enterprises Publishing

1325 6th Ave S #5 Payette, Idaho 83661

This collection of poetry reflects the views of the poet and is not representative of the views or opinions of Rodent Enterprises Publishing.

The following poems appeared previously in the listed journals

Abbey - Wrung Out

Arnezella - Recycling Wine Bottles in Your Behalf, The World has gone mad, Years After Round 12

Censored Poets - Throat by 8's

Conceit Magazine - Corks and Drowning, Ode to Laura Brown

The Endicott Review - Fighting the Undertow

Hazmat Literary Review - Angie

Heyday - Bent, Spaces in a Parallel Universe

Indigo Rising - Halos and Madness

March Street Press - The Falling Performance, The Widow

Midwest Poetry Review - Happy

Nerve Cowboy - Anywhere Town

Poesia - History Erupts

The Puckerbrush Review - Dresses in a Hovel, Gaps

Silver Blade - The Night

Struggle - The Coal Miner

The Tower Journal - Lady in Waiting, Pushing it down

Vox Poetica - Insomnia

Voyager - Adastra Press - 2010 - Anywhere Town, Angie, Wrung out, Little Schizophrenic Girl, Corn Tomorrow, Fighting the Undertow, The World Has Gone Mad, History Erupts, Happy

Copyright © 2011 Rodent Enterprises Publishing: Cover Design: GittyUPgo Design Group and Rodent Enterprises Publishing

Library of Congress Control Number: 2011939741

ISBN-13: 978-0-9837142-0-0

ISBN-10: 0-983-71420-7

All Rights Reserved. No part of this book may be reproduced using any means without the express written consent of the publisher.

Printed in the United States of America

First Edition: 2011

Table of Contents

Introduction	7
Ode to Laura Brown (From the film "The Hours")	8
Because She was fearful of sharks	9
Dresses in a Hovel	10
Gaps	11
Halos and Madness	12
The Coal Miner	14
Spikes of Pain	15
Throat by 8's	16
Memorial Day 2007 with my Father	17
Picasso	19
Years After Round 12	20
Crash	21
Insomnia	22
Stain	23
The Grid	24
The Night	26
Recycling Wine Bottles in Your Behalf	27
She Wears a Coffin	28
You're Eye-Bent	29
Bacon, Smoke, and Blood	30
Refinishing	31
Angry Blizzard	32
Anywhere Town	33
Angie	34
Wrung Out	35
Breaking Away	37
Living in Oblivion	38
Corks and Drowning	39

The Widow	41
Veil	42
Trauma	43
Tears	44
Pushing it down	45
The Machinist	46
The Falling of a Performance	47
Bent	48
Devil	49
Home to No Money	50
Spaces in a Parallel Universe	51
The Apples	52
The Day	53
The Fire at Midnight	54
Little Schizophrenic Girl	55
Corn Tomorrow	57
Fighting the Undertow	59
The World Has Gone Mad	61
History Erupts	63
Happy	64
Knowing	65
Lady in Waiting	67

Introduction
by Heather Helmer

Rare is it for me to come across a single collection of poetry that speaks to me. You pick up a poetry book expecting one or two to truly resonate with your soul, while the rest may come close or may be enjoyable in themselves and you think, "I can see that, but..."

For me this is one of those books where I never think that anything falls short of the mark. Everything resonates with me and some experience in my life. Not a single time do I have to wonder what was felt or thought, or "now what did that mean?"

This collection never left me wondering for a single moment, as I saw my own life reflected in the poems and pages of this book. Some brought smiles, some brought tears, some brought back dark things hidden in my closet from days long past that had been forgotten as I got older and the monster stopped seeming as important. Some brought back memories as sharp as a knife, piercing my mind with things buried and rather forgotten.

We're all tied to the wheel my friends, and I hope that how the book affected me reaches something in all of you. And when the dark little creatures lurking in your head rear their head and demand attention, maybe for the first time in years, my hope is that this book shows you, we really are all the same.

We are all tied to the wheel of Karma, and in the end all we have is each other.

Heather Helmer
Editor
Rodent Enterprises Publishing
4 October 2011

Ode to Laura Brown

(From the film "The Hours")

My bed is my chamber.
I do not want
For anything but sleep -
A beautiful, intoxicating Novocain.

Let me drink you in
And dine in my dreams -
They shall not forsake
Me like the rest
That drop red, rose petals
At my doorsteps.

I will no longer battle
You nor he nor she.
I am eternally awake
In my exhausted skin,
But feast on sleep
Like a hungry dog
In a frost-laden night.

Dawnell Harrison

Because She Was Fearful of Sharks

A razor bit the tiny hairs
Off the top of her leg,

The clippers snapped off
More than enough fingernail.

And later, the vibrations
Of his dentistry tool dug deeper

Into her nerve,
While the song she could

Usually change the channel on
Was harping in the back.

She clutched the plastic protectors
On the arms of the white chair

As her toes curled inside
Of her brown leather boots.

She asked if she could
Wipe her mouth on the blue bib

That lay pinned on
Like a clothesline.

Dresses in a Hovel

I make dresses out
Of drapes. We are
Poor you know -
Who else would do
Such a thing?

I make dresses out
Of old blankets.
We eat bread
For breakfast, lunch,
And dinner.
Who else would do
Such a thing?

When the dresses
Are worn out
I still use them
For rags to clean
Our hovel.
Who else would do
Such a thing?

I make dresses
In our hovel -
I make dresses out
Of drapes.

Gaps

There are so many
Gaps in this house
And in my brain
I wonder how
I can fill them all in.
With putty, crumpets or
Tea, with nails or
Glue or you.

Halos and Madness

The Gods are squeaky
Clean and I am
Laden with dirt -
Their halos and harps
And my mayhem
And madness.

I do not recoil
From my horror,
I have lived
There for years
And it has settled.

Love is the Gods
Undoing, an undoing
Of sweet nothings -
I can hear them

Echoing the night
Away - telling stories
Of hearts, love potions,
And a general high
Of epic proportions.

I have suffered
The violence of man
And will no longer
Be silent, no longer

Dawnell Harrison

Be silent, no longer
Be silent.

The Coal Miner

Heavy motes of black dust
Engulf the coal miner's lungs -
Even with a sturdy white mask
To keep out
The locust dark coal specks.

Arms heavy as a bronze statue,
Legs aching like a broken lover's heart
Piercing straight to his soul.
It is in his ruby red blood -
His Father was a
Headstrong coal miner too.

A prince of the underground
And hands as black
As bats, he rises above
And lays down another stroke
Of his weighty coal pick.

Dawnell Harrison

<u>Spikes of Pain</u>

Spikes of pain
Infiltrate my eyes,
My bones,
My flesh,
As if hot daggers
Are being thrown about -

Some landing
In my brain,
Some standing
And watching
The strain -

Always peering
With eyes made
Of black, sticky pearls
And pupils that
Widen, widen, widen
And knowing when I'll move.

Throat by 8's

The tiger lily's
Dotted throat
Raises oranges into a pale
Light,
Into the dark night, as yon
Lovers
Dream upon its primitive
Beauty and its hot colors.

I dream upon the neck
Of yesterday and
Ravage about the future
While living plainly
In the moments of now -
The seconds of my
Discontented
Demeanor, my discontented nights.

Dawnell Harrison

<u>Memorial Day 2007 with my Father</u>

Kept it locked up until,
Like fractured glass,

Small shards came spilling
Down my cheeks -

Dead relatives and
The story about

The cocker spaniel
That you witnessed get hit by a car

Near the cemetery,
The one your Mother

Cried at everyday
Because her husband, your Father,

Had blown his brains out
With a large gun and not left a note,

Leaving a wake
Of sadness and anger

And part of your legacy.
We placed wild, thorny roses

The Fire Behind My Eyes

By the graves of
Viola Harrison
George Harrison

Albert Harrison
Clara Harrison

Dorthy Simpson
Dutch and Grace.

Dawnell Harrison

Picasso

I'm rearranging my eyes
Like Picasso and feel
As if my feet really are
On the top of my head.

It's not like a headache,
But more like a terminally
Pounding migraine that
Eats at my nerves and
Wears a hat for show.

It's enough to drive the meek mad,
But I choose to go loony instead.

The Fire Behind My Eyes

Years After Round 12

Throughout your Father's house,
My mind questions your recollection of Mother

Shoved into Idaho walls and fists,
Stony bruises last for weeks -

Do you push those days
Onto a far off antique moon,

The one you send me to everyday,
Silently.

Crash

I crash into
Humpty Dumpty's pieces.

Pick me up
Bit by bit,
Unglued.

Too easy with tears,
You let them
Cascade down my face
Without lifting
A tissue.
I expect that.

Don't act dumb.
You know this
Winter routine.

Insomnia

The red roses have closed
Their buds and said good night
And only my mind speed is awake.

The night sky heckles me
With its spotted illuminating stars
And intoxicating blackness as if to say
I dare you to fall asleep
With all of this beauty above you.

I am vertical now. They say
To get up if you can't sleep
And read, but the words drag
In my mind in unsteady circles.

I am immune to books at this
Thieving hour. Maybe I'll
Count pigs instead of sheep.

Dawnell Harrison

<u>Stain</u>

Her memory left
A stain that I
Can't get up.
She's embedded
In the carpet
And your brain.

When it rains
It floods -
When the wind
Blows it knocks
Over trees and
The birds have
Nowhere to hide
Like my tattered soul.

Her smile left
A stain that I
Can't get up.
She's your
Quiet muse -
Still waiting
For you to knock
On her door
Once again.

The Grid

They lit me up like
A New York City grid.
I told them that
They shall not
Have the better of me.

Pulsating waves of electricity
Swept through me like
A torrid thunder storm.
The rubber piece
That they shoved
In my mouth
Did not begin
To thwart my
Haunted screams.

There is nothing
Behind my eyes -
If you look closely
You will see
Black sticky pearls
For pupils.
I shuffle down
The hallways in my
Pale, blue slippers repeating
That they shall not
Have the better of me,

Dawnell Harrison

The better of me,
The better of me.

The Night

The night rolls out
Like blackberry thickets -
Prickly and foreboding.

The earth smells
Of fresh rain
From the thunderstorm
That crackled like
Wood thrown
Onto a campfire.

Nobody is sleeping -
Everyone has lost
Track of time
As if they are
Under water.

The flower petals
Are as bleached as death.
I flounder in bed
And try to cast
My dream aside.

Dawnell Harrison

Recycling Wine Bottles in Your Behalf

My blood moves thickly
Within the noisy silence
Of this one toothbrush
Apartment.

I drink pensively for you
Inside my bottle of Dry Riesling
And climb out within an hour -
Craggy fingers now empty.

If I were young
I would draw your name repeatedly,
Hearts etched amorously,
Replace my last name with yours -
Tangled in liquid fairy tales.

She Wears a Coffin

Moments of numbness
Rise into days
Then weeks
Without you.

Death is the sheath
She covers herself in,
Scarf and gloves alike.

Her voice echoes
Blankly like
No vowels or consonants
Had been spoken at all.

Empty as a cupboard glass
Her heart winces and groans
Without you.

Dawnell Harrison

You're Eye-bent

You're eye-bent
On being annihilating
And asking rhetorical questions
Just to seem smart.

You resent my smile
Like a dog detests a cat
And don't economize
On your insults, however
Underhanded they ring.

Your mailbox is full
Of junk mail -
It makes you believe
That you are very important
To someone or something -
Oh how the moon
Knows that you are not.

You're eye-bent
On being annihilating
And asking rhetorical questions
Just to seem smart.

Bacon, Smoke, and Blood

The bacon spats and
Spits its grease in

The pan like a campfire
Cackling into the

Smokey night air.
The smoke rises up

Deadening the stars,
But the beauty of

The campfire flames
Keeps us transfixed and struck

Like a coyote on the
Freeway at midnight.

Dawnell Harrison

Refinishing

So your couch is velvet
But your touch needs
Refinishing,

A touch made from
A life gone unnoticed
And unplanned.

So you drink vodka martinis
But your touch needs
Refinishing,

A touch as harsh
As sandpaper, a touch
Unfulfilled and
Anonymous.

So your mouth is full
Of diamonds and gold
But your touch needs
Refinishing,

A touch as raw
As burnt nerves and
An isolated star
Falling from the sky.

Angry Blizzard

Years of an angry
Earth is falling down
With its constant
Snow. I can't recall
If it has snowed for
3 weeks or 41 years now.

The snow buckles
The house and
The power lines as
If its weight
Is true and
Angst-ridden.

Trees dressed
In white stand
Out in alleys
Over an unexpected
Solitude.

A woman turns
Around there -
Her small tracks
Engrained upon
The earth.

Dawnell Harrison

<u>Anywhere Town</u>

The train station
Was as empty
As a cupboard bowl
And I examined
The grain of the
Wooden bench I
Sat on near
The vacant coffee stand.

It felt very smooth as if it
Had been painstakingly
Lacquered for many years.

I was taking
The next train
To Anywhere-but-here
Town. A town I think we've all
Wanted to visit at
One stage or another.

The make-up barely
Hid the bluish-green bruises
On my left eye,
So I wore large
Sunglasses in my
Dark surrender to the night.
Anywhere-but-Here Town.

Angie

Angie is dancing
On the table.

Easy to say she's had
One too many.

You know who your
Friends are on nights
Like this.

Angie likes pills.
Pink, green, white, orange,
And the entire rainbow really.
She forgets what some
Of them are for and just "wings it,"
As she says.

She's been pushed
Too far today.

She'll forget it all tomorrow
And I'll recall everything.

Long taxi ride.

Dawnell Harrison

<u>Wrung Out</u>

Once you've entered
My vortex

Expect
Tornadoes

Floods
And hurricanes.

Don't expect
Quiet nights

Lying side by side.
Expect my hurricane

To pick you up
And swirl

You around
Like a dark horse

In the night.
Isn't that how

We all want it,
A challenge

The Fire Behind My Eyes

Until it becomes
too tiring

And you're
Wrung out

Like a wet rag
In a dirty sink

That you can
Never fully get clean.

Dawnell Harrison

Breaking Away

You're breaking away
From me like
Crackling icicles
From my doorstep eaves.

You're breaking away
From me like
Gravel separating
Tires from the earth
When you drive away.

You're breaking away
From me like
Rain from a thunderstorm
Pounding down on me
Like a jackhammer.

You're breaking away
From me like
The sunset slowly lowering
Until it's gone,
And you just don't see
It anymore.

Living in Oblivion

Living in oblivion -
A forgetting or having forgotten.

At 40 I am living in oblivion -
Hardly noticed in the crowd.
It is no longer my time.
The younger girls fly like kites
And I stop to behold their beauty.

Living in oblivion -
A forgetting or having forgotten.

Fly your kites in greens and blues
Daughters of the Gods
And shine with gilded light
Upon your honey blonde hair.

Corks and Drowning

The clouds were just
Passing by the moon
When the ocean
Spat me out
As clean as a cork
From a bottle of champagne.

I suppose drowning was not my forte
Or the sea did not
Want me on that
Warm summer's eve.

I got tired of breathing -
It had become a job
And I rationalized
That the air was as
Polluted as a
Coal miner's lungs.

It was my duty
To try to die again
Since I always knew
That the Gods
Wanted me more
Than this tainted
And flawed planet.

The Fire Behind My Eyes

I could hear
The humming of angels
Drawing me in like
A new lover casting
Waves of seduction
On my ruby, red heart.

Dawnell Harrison

The Widow

She wears death
Like a silent syllable -
Words do not consume her.

She is quiet
Like a frozen lake
At midnight and wears
Black as if it
Were her own.

She does not hear
The voice of God
Or her dead relatives.
She can barely breathe.

She wears death
Like a silent syllable.

Veil

A black veil
Clings to my face,
Somebody has died
And I am searching
For the ashes -
Bone fragments and all.

I cannot walk or run,
I am rooted in the snow.
It would take a sleigh
Of horses to set me free.

Fog rolls out the night
And I cannot stand
Still with this black veil
Hovering about my face.

Dawnell Harrison

Trauma

Sunshine turns the hours
Into a darkness
Where not even muffled trumpets
Can be heard.

Your demon boat
Has set sail
And stony bruises
Don't cover up easily.

Silver dorsal fins that have earlier
Broken the water's surface
Now wait for a
Better time to emerge.

The boat is crashing
Into waves of trauma
And I retreat into myself
Like a salty sea creature
With cracked hands over my face.

It doesn't help.
Your demon boat is on the rise.

The Fire Behind My Eyes

<u>Tears</u>

If we lived in a universe
Without tears,
How would bruises
Find a place to rest.

If we lived in a Universe
Without tears,
How would scars
Find a space
To etch themselves into.

If we lived in a universe
Without tears,
How would the
Broken-hearted
Find the bones
Buried six feet under.

Dawnell Harrison

Pushing it Down

Tried to fake it,
Too jaded to pretend
For one more second
That living this life
Isn't bleeding me
From the inside out,
Keep pushing it down.

I've given up the drama
And traded it in for
Hermitville. It's a nice place
To live - Nobody there
To criticize me but myself.
Keep pushing it down.

Living in this city
Of one is really
Oh so lovely!
My old cat
With two torn ears
Gets my undivided attention
As I keep pushing it down.

The Machinist

The machinist
Works graveyard
And without stopping.
Cigarettes are his friend
After work.

He's hard-nosed,
Brimming with adrenaline,
And oozing
With the smell of beer
From the night before.

His hands are
Coal fire black
From the grease
And hard work.

He feels like
He's coming undone,
Similar to one of the old,
Rusty machines
That he works on at night.

He knows that it is coming but,
The machines don't
Stop for human frailty.

The Falling of a Performance

Losing my soul bit by bit
Is a performance.
Like most everything else,
I do it exceedingly poorly.

I may possess an ill-fated
Profession like a working girl who
Is bound and tied to survive
From the dollars of hundreds
Of dullard, gold-ringed men.

My essence needs to be restrung
Like a degenerating guitar
Gathering dust the way
A cobweb takes over
A corner lot.

I do believe that vertigo
Has caught me in its
Hurried fists like a
Firefighter rescuing a child
And making the world right again,
If only for a fleeting instant.

Bent

The day was bent
Like a sheet of metal

And drifted in
With pockets of rain.

I contemplated my
To do list with a scent

Of contempt and
Drank my vanilla coffee slowly.

The day tasted like
Twisted steel

And felt like
Old bread in my pantry.

I tried to think
Good thoughts,

But they faded as I
Looked at my peach-colored

Nails that were chipped
Like an antique teacup.

Dawnell Harrison

<u>Devil</u>

The day develops slowly
Like an impending rain storm

On the heels of the devil.
The day shouts into the wind

Blazing through the skies
Like a comet through space.

The day never apologizes
For its fury that rides as if

On a wild horse in Montana -
Its black mane breaking
Through the air.

The Fire Behind My Eyes

Home to No Money

There's TV radiation
To fill up my head,
But I choose
To read psychology
Books instead.

I live on bread
And honey -
This is the way home
To no money.
I stumble over

Flat ground -
The day spins
Around and around
As if I am
On a cheap carnival ride.

Close your brown eyes
And spit out your story.
I will let it
Drift away like an epiphany
That just passed me by.

Dawnell Harrison

Spaces in a Parallel Universe

Home is a space
In time
With a parallel universe
Where the others reside

In the reality of wants,
Of needs,
Of misfortunes
And they burn

Past midnight
Into the ears
Of those dreaming
In colors and 3D.

Nobody is home.
The have all lost
Track of time
As if under water.

Home is a space
In time
With a parallel universe
Where the others reside.

The Apples

Apples were falling
From the almost barren trees
In the summer heat

Like fireflies
Darting in and out
Of my illuminated porch.

The air was buzzing
With the hopes
Of the forgotten

In the cemetery
Where their bones
Rise up and break

Like a chandelier
From a high ceiling.
My thoughts

Wear thick clogs -
The sounds of shoe heels clopping
Echo down an empty hallway.

Dawnell Harrison

The Day

The day blew in
Like dried leaves
That crunched
Under my feet.

My ideas wore clogs -
The echo sounds
From shoe heels clopping.
My dreams were

Tossed aside like
A child's toy
In the back yard.
The flowers hung

Their heads as if
They were mourners
At a funeral.
I dreamt a dream

That was out
Of my reach
Like a hot air balloon
Waving its hot colors
In the robin's egg blue sky.

The Fire at Midnight

His eyes burnt a hole
Into the maze of my life -
There was always
A fire at midnight.

His eyes bore into my soul
Like a determined priest
Performing an exorcism.
There was always

A fire at midnight.
His eyes bled
Through an ebony-laden sky -
There was always

A fire at midnight.
His eyes set upon me
As if I were merchandise.
There was always
A fire at midnight.

Dawnell Harrison

Little Schizophrenic Girl

We love our little schizophrenic girl,
All bundled up in shackles
And secluded in barns
With bright red doors.

We love our little schizophrenic girl,
She hides behind apple trees
Laden with heavy sweet fruit,
Too sweet too eat.

Today she was wearing
A black and white striped Jackie-O scarf
Around her head and
A pair of big black sunglasses.
What an idiot!

We love our little schizophrenic girl,
She talks to cats
And we think they understand her.
They are always meowing back
so we just assume,
disquieting as it seems.

We love our little schizophrenic girl,
All Blake-like with her
Mind forged manacles crap.
What does that mean?

The Fire Behind My Eyes

"Look it up," she says.
It's Blake, William Blake.

We love our little schizophrenic girl.

Dawnell Harrison

Corn Tomorrow

Dragging feet
And slippers create
That scruff-scruff sound,
So annoying yet mother's milk
Familiar. Hungry again.

Locked up,
Scooting down
Your hall of existence.
Warped, sick, yet you -
So all is peachy
Within your mind's apple.

Fatty, sticky, ugly food,
Yet eat eat eat.
What else is on the menu?

Your best friend
Just pulled the TV
Off of the stand
For no good reason
Say the nurses.
You laugh.
A good chuckle for the day.
Oh that Bruce!

Nothing but scrabble

The Fire Behind My Eyes

        And a bunch of screw-ups
        Singing old Vincent Minnelli tunes
        Because those Minnelli songs
        Are so gosh darned perfect.

        Ask for corn instead
        Of green beans tomorrow.

Dawnell Harrison

Fighting the Undertow
(For Sylvia)

It takes less than death
To kill one woman's soul.
Sylvia crawled under her lovely house
To die undiscovered.

Always fighting the undertow -
Is it DNA or just the everyday
That makes you let go before you
Go down down down below.

I heard you, I saw you
Going down down down below.
I couldn't help you
Because I had already been
Below for so long my dear,
And was looking up at you from down below.
Always fighting the undertow.

The muck and mire and blackness
Like the darkest perfect little black pearls
Leave a trail of normal existence.

How do you clean yourself
From the inside out?
Maybe if God reaches down and
Scoops me up and kisses

The Fire Behind My Eyes

The top of my head with light beams.
(I'll tell him to scoop you up and kiss you too.)
Now we can rest.
No longer fighting the undertow.

Dawnell Harrison

The World Has Gone Mad

The world has gone mad.
My only solace, like a sea creature
living its existence in a salty, safe shell,
Is to imagine swimming
Amongst them as a mermaid in
Silky blues and greens.

The drug addicts
Across the street
Have finally been evicted.
I heard a woman screaming
A wretched helter-skelter scream
At 2:40 A.M. about three months ago.
I knew where it was emanating from and
Did not get up to investigate.
I imagine she would like to be a mermaid.

A brown dog was mutilated by a car
In front of my house
About two months ago.
The jerk that ran over her
Scurried away
Like an 18-year-old
Enlisting in the military
Who has just discovered he is a father.

The dog's bloody eyes, face

The Fire Behind My Eyes

Still drag in my mind
In unsteady circles
When I can't sleep.
She can be a mermaid beside me in
Silky blues and greens.

Dawnell Harrison

<u>History Erupts</u>

My doctor's wife has been stealing
Money from him. I declare
That I have become a hermit.
We confide in each other
I suppose instead of reaching
For the emptiness of a drink
or the instant rush a cookie provides.

I am looking for another job,
Certain already that I will hate it
As much as the previous one.
My next boss will not be
A control freak like the last,
But I am sure his deficiencies
Will rear-up into a tormented head
And come down on me like
A judge's gavel to the hard wood.

I've been thinking of the past, youth.
Recalling fresh days without resentment and
Laughing as if time had stopped
And only that moment was pure.

The Fire Behind My Eyes

Happy

I thought moving
To a new house
Would make me happy.
I had temporarily forgotten
That I'd be bringing myself along.

Dawnell Harrison

<u>Knowing</u>

I knew that
You knew

That I knew
That you never

Had an original
Thought in your

Tender brain.
Your thoughts

Bent into the day
Like twisted sheet metal

At the idea
Of creating

Something out of nothing
As if the air

Could be filled
With newness

And a beauty
Only seen

The Fire Behind My Eyes

In blood, red roses
That opened at midnight.

Lady In Waiting

The lady in waiting
Cries hushed tears
At night after she's
Waited on the royalty
As if they were Gods.
She'd like to uproot them -
Corsets, teacakes,
And all.

The sky's done for
As she gazes out
Of her small window
Into the night of her
Own undoing. Another
Night where nobody
Will serenade her,
Another night indeed.

Poverty begins to weigh
Itself as an option.
Too many days of
Yes madam and yes sir,
No madam and no sir.

Although she would be
Penniless, she could
Unhook the stars
As if they were her own.

www.ingramcontent.com/pod-product-compliance
Lightning Source LLC
Chambersburg PA
CBHW032100150426
43194CB00006B/598